SHIRLEY HOMES

T0139363

AN
LITHUANIAN CASE

You can find private investigators like Shirley Homes anywhere in the world. Put the words 'private investigator' into a Google search on the internet, and you get more than 6,800,000 hits.

Private investigators do all kinds of detective jobs. Perhaps they look for information about a person . . . Is that their real name? Where do they live? Where did they live before that? How old are they? Do they really have a university degree from Harvard, USA? Perhaps the job is watching somebody . . . Where do they go? Who do they meet? What do they talk about? Perhaps a business is losing money, but nobody understands why. A private investigator can listen and watch, day and night, and find an answer.

So what is the Lithuanian Case? It is a missing persons case. There is a missing daughter, Carrie Williams, aged fifteen. There is a new boyfriend, from Lithuania. There is a crying mother, there is an angry father, there is an unhappy little brother.

Carrie left her family home in London five weeks ago. Carrie's mother wants Shirley Homes to find her. Shirley knows London very well – but she also understands people . . .

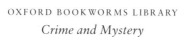

OXFORD BOOKWORMS LIBRARY
Crime and Mystery

Shirley Homes and the Lithuanian Case

Stage 1 (400 headwords)

Series Editor: Jennifer Bassett
Founder Editor: Tricia Hedge
Activities Editors: Jennifer Bassett and Christine Lindop

JENNIFER BASSETT

Shirley Homes
and the
Lithuanian Case

Illustrated by
Nelson Evergreen

OXFORD UNIVERSITY PRESS

OXFORD
UNIVERSITY PRESS

Great Clarendon Street, Oxford, OX2 6DP, United Kingdom

Oxford University Press is a department of the University of Oxford.
It furthers the University's objective of excellence in research, scholarship,
and education by publishing worldwide. Oxford is a registered trade
mark of Oxford University Press in the UK and in certain other countries

© Oxford University Press 2012

The moral rights of the author have been asserted

First published in Oxford Bookworms 2012

10

ISBN: 978 0 19 479369 8

A complete recording of this Bookworms edition of
Shirley Homes and the Lithuanian Case is also available

Printed in China

Word count (main text): 5,856 words

For more information on the Oxford Bookworms Library,
visit www.oup.com/bookworms

ACKNOWLEDGEMENTS

Illustrations by: Nelson Evergreen/The Bright Agency

CONTENTS

CHAPTER 1

A missing daughter

Somebody is ringing my office doorbell. It's ten past nine on a Monday morning. That's early for a client to call. But perhaps this is going to be a good week. Last week business was not very good. I need some new clients.

I look at my computer. I want to see the person before I open the door. The little camera over the door shows me a woman in a raincoat. About forty, maybe. Not rich. The raincoat is a cheap one, from the street market. She's carrying a newspaper, the *Putney Gazette*.

The camera shows me a woman in a raincoat.

I hit the 'open door' button on the wall. The door opens, and the woman comes in.

'Are you the private investigator? Shirley Homes?' she asks. She looks around the office, probably looking for someone older.

'I am.' I use my older person voice. 'Please sit down, Mrs . . . er . . .'

'Williams. Edith Williams,' she says. She sits down in my best chair, and looks around the office again, still looking for that older person.

'How can I help you, Mrs Williams?' I say. 'What's your problem?'

She looks at me then, and the trouble in her face is clear.

'Do you find people?' she says. 'Can you find my daughter? She left home five weeks ago. Just walked out. Took all her things, and walked out. And not a word from her. No phone calls. Not even a text. Nothing.'

Edith Williams is nearly crying now.

'Why?' I ask.

I'm careful. Family problems can be dangerous. You open a door, and all kinds of dark and horrible things come out. And when those dark and horrible things are out, you can never put them back in again.

Edith Williams is still trying not to cry.

'Why, Mrs Williams?' I say again. 'Why did your daughter leave home? Was there an argument?'

'Not with me, no. It's her father, he . . .' Now she really is crying. Five weeks of crying, all in two minutes in my office.

I get her a cup of coffee, and sit on a chair next to her.

'Tell me all about it, Mrs Williams. Take your time.'

'Tell me all about it, Mrs Williams. Take your time.'

The daughter, Carrie, is fifteen, I learn. She likes boys, has lots of boyfriends, doesn't listen to her parents. So what's new? Many fifteen-year-old girls are like that.

But the new boyfriend, Edith Williams says, is older, and he's not English. He's a foreigner, from Lithuania.

I remember my Ukrainian grandmother, my Greek mother. Foreigners.

'Is that a problem for you?' I ask. 'A foreigner?'

'Not for me, but it is for my husband,' Edith Williams says. 'He doesn't like foreigners. They come here, he says, they take our jobs, they take our houses, they take our money. And they can't speak English. He gets very angry about it. He says some horrible things to Carrie. "I don't want this foreigner in my house," he says, and Carrie goes crazy. She calls her father some horrible names, and he gets really angry. He's shouting, and Carrie's crying. They don't stop for hours.'

Edith Williams stops for a second. She can still hear the shouting and the crying, I think.

'And what happened next?' I ask quietly.

'The next day,' Mrs Williams says, 'Carrie left. Early in the morning, before we all got up. She left a letter.'

'Have you got the letter?' I ask.

'Yes, I have.' She gives the letter to me, and I read it quickly. An angry letter, from an angry fifteen-year-old. Nothing useful. I give the letter back to her.

'I asked all her friends,' Mrs Williams says. 'Everyone.

'Carrie calls her father some horrible names, and he gets really angry. He's shouting, and Carrie's crying.'

They didn't know – or they didn't want to tell me. And she's stopped going to school.'

'What about the police?' I ask.

'I can't go to the police. My husband doesn't want to see her again. We can't even say her name at home.'

'We? Who's we?'

'Me and Darren. He's Carrie's little brother. He's ten. He's very unhappy about all this.'

I must meet Darren. Ten-year-old boys can be very useful. They see and hear a lot.

Edith Williams looks at me with her red eyes. 'Can you find her for me? I just want to know she's all right. And this boyfriend, this Lithuanian . . . What's he like? How old is he? What does he do? Is he kind? Is he the right person for my little girl?'

I take the job. I ask for a photograph of Carrie, the names of friends, the school, mobile phone numbers.

'Can I talk to Darren?' I ask.

'Yes, we can meet him after school,' Edith Williams says. 'But please don't come to my house. Please. My husband . . .'

'I understand,' I say. 'I can text you when I have some news.'

She doesn't know the name of the Lithuanian boyfriend. That's *really* helpful. There are thousands of Lithuanians in London. Finding one young man without a name in thousands of people? How easy is that!

CHAPTER 2

Help from friends

I begin with Carrie, of course. I have a name and a photograph, and a school. I meet Darren when he comes out of school, and we go to Carrie's school. We sit in my car and watch the students when they leave.

'That's Janice – look!' says Darren. 'The girl with long black hair. She's very friendly with Carrie. And that's

We sit in my car and watch the students when they leave.

'Can you find my sister?' Darren says.

Kim, next to her. I like Kim. She's funny, she makes me laugh. Ooh, and that's Ant. See – the one with very short hair and black clothes.'

'Ant? What name is that? Anthea?'

'Don't know,' says Darren. 'She's just Ant.'

I take a quick photo of the three girls, and then I take Darren for a pizza to say thank you.

'Can you find my sister?' he says. 'It's horribly quiet at home without her. Nobody ever laughs now. Mum cries all night. I hear her.'

I look at his small boy face. 'Yup. I can find her.'

That evening I phone my friend in the police. He's a detective – Detective Sergeant Saheed Patel.

'Hi, Saheed, how are you?'

'Fine. What's new with you?' Saheed says. 'Are you working on a case?'

'Yes, I've got a missing persons case – a missing girl. Her mother came to me today. The girl left home five weeks ago after an argument with her father about her boyfriend . . . a Lithuanian boyfriend.'

'How old is the girl?' Saheed asks.

'Fifteen.'

'Oh dear.' Saheed is not surprised. 'Every day we get missing persons reports – do you know how many?'

'No. Tell me. How many?'

'The police in Britain get about 1,000 reports every day,' Saheed says. 'And nearly one third of those are young people between the ages of fifteen and seventeen. When did the mother make the report to the police?'

'She didn't. The girl's father doesn't want to see her again,' I say. 'So, no police, no missing persons report, and no looking for her. That's what the mother told me.'

'OK. Be careful, Shirley. The girl's only fifteen. She can't get married before she's sixteen, and the law says—'

'I know all that, Saheed! I know the law!'

'Of course you do. Sorry.' There's a smile in Saheed's voice. 'So what do you want from me?'

'Can you help with the Lithuanian boyfriend?' I say. 'Where do I look for him? Can you give me some names? People to talk to.'

'Maybe. But there are about 200,000 Lithuanians in

There's a smile in Saheed's voice.

London. When do you want this? I have work to do, you know.'

'I'm going to try the girl's school friends first,' I say. 'Can you do it in a day or two? Text me when you have something.'

'OK. Bye now.'

The next day at four o'clock, I'm outside Carrie's school. I have my photo of the three girls, and I soon see them. They're standing, all three of them, in the street, looking at their mobile phones and laughing. I walk over to them.

'Hi, guys,' I say. 'You're friends of Carrie Williams, right? I need your help.'

'Carrie Williams?' says the girl called Ant. 'Who's she?'

I watch the girls' faces. They know Carrie, all right. And they know she's missing. But how much do they know?

'Ah, come on,' I say. 'You're Carrie's best friends. I'm looking for her. I need to find her.'

'And who are you?' asks the girl called Janice.

I give them my card.

SHIRLEY HOMES

PRIVATE INVESTIGATOR

The girl called Kim laughs. 'Shirley Homes? Are you the granddaughter of Sherlock Holmes or something?'

I smile. I get this all the time, again and again. And again. 'Great-great-granddaughter. He lived in the 1890s.'

'Wow! Really? That is awesome!' says Kim.

Janice and Ant laugh. 'Kim, you idiot! Sherlock Holmes wasn't a *real* person. He's just a detective in stories on television.'

'Er, and in books,' I say. 'The books were first.'

The girls look at me, and their faces are more friendly now.

'OK, Shirley Homes, great-great-granddaughter of Sherlock,' says Ant. 'How can we help you? Who are you looking for? What was her name again?'

Ant is going to be difficult, I can see that. She's a good friend of Carrie's, and she's not going to talk.

'Do you have mothers?' I say. 'All three of you?'

The girls stare at me. 'Of course we have mothers,' says Janice. 'What are you talking about?'

'Do you love your mothers? Do your mothers love

Ant gives Kim an angry look. 'We don't know Carrie Williams!'

you?' I say. 'Well, listen. Carrie's mother loves her daughter. And now Carrie's mother can't sleep at night. She doesn't eat. She cries about Carrie all the time. She wants to know that *Carrie is all right*. Can you understand that? She just wants to *know*.'

Kim looks at me with big eyes. 'Oh, poor Mrs Williams!' she says.

Ant gives her an angry look. 'We don't know Carrie Williams!' she says. 'Remember?'

Janice looks at me. 'Give us a minute,' she says. 'We need to talk.'

They move away, turn their backs to me, and talk quietly. I can't hear them. Then they come back to me.

'OK,' says Ant. 'What do you want?'

'You know Café Nero in Putney High Street?' I say. 'Tell Carrie this. I'm going to be in Café Nero at 18.30 tomorrow evening, and 18.30 the evening after that. I want to see her and talk to her. I want to know she's alive and well. That's all. Then I can tell her mother, and Mrs Williams can stop crying all night.'

'OK,' Ant says. 'We got it.'

'Thanks, guys,' I say. 'See you around.'

'See you,' they say.

CHAPTER 3

Talking to Carrie

Carrie doesn't come the first evening. I sit there for two hours, and drink a lot of coffee. Five big cups, black, no sugar. It's a good thing I like coffee.

But she comes the second evening. I'm sitting with my back to the wall, watching the door. Through the café window I see Ant in her black clothes. She's walking past, slowly, looking into the café. A minute or two later Carrie comes in, and walks over to my table. Red hair, green eyes, no smile. I stand up.

'Hi, Carrie. I'm Shirley Homes. Thanks for coming. Have a seat. Can I get you a coffee, or a tea?'

I'm using my head teacher voice. *Right, girls, sit down. Open your books. Get to work.* I don't want Carrie to have time to think.

She doesn't want coffee, or tea. She wants to have an argument.

'I'm not going home,' she says. 'So you can forget that. I don't need my family. I have a new life now.'

I watch her face, and she stares back at me with angry green eyes. I don't think Carrie is in trouble. Carrie knows what she wants, and Carrie gets what she wants. I think Carrie *makes* trouble. I begin to feel sorry for the boyfriend.

Carrie comes in, and walks over to my table.

'Why are you here, Carrie?' I say. 'What did your friends say to you?'

She doesn't answer, just looks at me.

'Did they tell you about your mum – crying all night because her little girl is living on the streets, because her little girl is taking drugs, because her little girl is in big, big trouble—'

Suddenly, Carrie has a lot to say. 'I'm NOT living on

the streets!' she shouts at me. 'And I don't do drugs – I
NEVER do drugs! Who told you all this? It's NOT TRUE!'

People in the café turn their heads to look at us. I smile
around at everybody. A smile to say, *Everything's fine here.
Just a big sister, little sister argument. Happens all the
time. Enjoy your coffee, have a nice day . . .*

People in the café turn their heads to look at us.

I look back at Carrie's angry face.

'But your mum doesn't know that,' I say quietly. 'At night, when she can't sleep, she thinks about those things. You're only fifteen, Carrie, and it's a big bad world out there. Of course your mum is afraid for you.'

Carrie looks down at the table. 'Yeah. Well . . .' She looks up. 'But I'm OK. I'm fine. You can tell her that.'

'Why don't *you* tell her?' I say. 'Call her. Text her.'

Carrie stares at me. 'Who sent you?' she says. 'Mum? Or was it my dad?'

'Your mum.'

'Look, I'm not texting mum, because I don't want my dad to know. I don't want to see him again, ever.'

'We're not talking about your dad,' I say quickly. 'I know all about your dad. We're talking about your mum. And your mum needs to know you're all right. But she needs to hear it from *you*, not me. She texts you every day, you know. And you never text back. Never.'

Carrie looks away. 'I got a new mobile, and changed my number. I never got her texts.'

I laugh. 'Very good, Carrie. You read detective stories, right? Always change your mobile when you don't want people to find you. Dangerous things, mobile phones.'

Carrie nearly smiles. 'Tomas says—' she begins, then stops.

'Is Tomas your boyfriend?' I say. 'The one from Lithuania? Are you still with him?'

'Of course I'm still with him!' Carrie is angry again. 'I love him and he loves me. We're in love!'

I try not to smile. How wonderful to be fifteen, and in love for the first time!

'That's great,' I say. 'I'm happy for you. But please, please text your mum. Tell her you're all right.'

'OK,' says Carrie. 'This evening.' She looks at her watch and stands up. 'I must go. I'm meeting someone.'

'Thanks for coming, Carrie. And remember that text.'

She walks out of the café, and fifteen seconds later I'm following her. She's walking down the High Street, maybe to the bus station. I've got a minute, but I must be quick.

A private investigator always needs to carry a big bag. I stop by a shop window, and open my bag. Three seconds later, I'm wearing a blue T-shirt over my red T-shirt. In another five seconds, I have a wig on, and my short black hair is now long blond hair. Now I'm walking away from the shop window, and I'm wearing glasses. My big brown bag is now inside a small black backpack. No time to change the shoes. Carrie is a long way down the street. I walk fast, nearly running, and watch her red head in front of me.

When I get to the bus station, I can't see her at first, and walk quickly past all the people waiting. She's there, waiting for the number 71 bus. I wait too, about twenty metres away, and I'm reading the evening newspaper with great interest. (A private investigator always has today's newspaper in their bag.) But Carrie doesn't look round.

When the bus comes, Carrie goes upstairs. This is good news for me because I can sit downstairs, at the

I'm reading the evening newspaper with great interest.

back of the bus. I can see Carrie when she gets off, but she can't see me.

It's a short bus ride, only ten minutes. Carrie gets off the bus, and turns left into a small street. I'm thirty metres behind her. Carrie looks round, once, and sees someone with blond hair, in a blue T-shirt, and glasses. She doesn't know me.

There are six bells by the door with names next to them.

Halfway down the street, she crosses the road and goes into a big old house. I walk past the house, not too fast, not too slow. I can't follow her into the house because there are no other people around. You can only hide easily when there are lots of people around.

I take the next right, walk for ten minutes, then turn around and come back. This time I walk to the front door of the big house. There are six bells by the door with names next to them. It's a house with six different apartments. I look at the names, but there isn't a 'Williams' next to any bell. Well, of course not. She's living with her Lithuanian boyfriend. I look at the names again . . . John Ozumba, K. Brown, Lili Sardelli, R. Varnaite, T. Grigas, M. M. Westerbrook.

Varnaite and Grigas . . . Lithuanian names, I think. Tomas Grigas, perhaps?

You can't stand in a quiet street and watch a house. Everybody looks at you and says, 'Who's that woman? What's she doing?' But you can watch a house from a car. People often sit in cars, waiting for somebody, having a sleep, checking their phone messages . . .

I go home, make some spaghetti for dinner, and text Edith Williams.

> Saw C today. She's fine.
> More tomorrow.

CHAPTER 4

The boyfriend

The next day I'm in the street in my car, opposite the house. I have a cup of coffee, a newspaper, and a lot of time. I want to see Tomas, and talk to him. Then I can make my report to Mrs Williams, and the job is finished.

At 17.45 Carrie walks down the street, and goes into the house. I'm watching carefully now. People are coming home from work . . . in cars, on bicycles, on foot. Lots to watch. Two people go into the house, a young woman and a short, older man with white hair.

At 18.25 a young man walks down the street. Tall, with dark hair. He walks to the front door, and in two seconds I'm out of the car, across the street, and standing behind him at the door.

He opens the door, and turns to look at me.

'Hi!' I say. 'OK to come in? I'm visiting Mike Westerbrook at number six.'

'Yes, that's OK,' the young man says. He holds the door open for me, and we walk up the stairs together.

'Nice and sunny today,' I say. 'But rain's coming in later, they say.'

'Mmm,' says the young man.

At the top of the stairs he turns to the door with number

4 on it, gets out his key, and opens the door. Suddenly, I run back to him.

'Hey, excuse me! Is this yours? It was on the floor.' In my hand I'm holding a weekly bus ticket. It's more than two months old, but he can't see that because I've got my hand over the date.

He looks at the ticket, and I look through the open

In two seconds I'm standing behind him at the door.

door of number 4 . . . and see Carrie in the room. Then I'm through the door and inside the apartment.

'Hey!' the young man shouts at me. 'What are you doing? Who are you? Get out!'

I turn to Carrie. 'Hello, Carrie,' I say. 'Did you text your mum last night?'

The young man is next to me now. 'Who *is* this?' he

'Hello, Carrie,' I say. 'Did you text your mum last night?'

says to Carrie. 'What's this about?' He stares at me angrily.

Carrie looks angry too. 'She's a private investigator,' she tells the young man. 'Mum sent her. I talked to her yesterday in the café. I told you, remember?'

'Ah!' The young man suddenly smiles. He has a very nice smile. 'How exciting! I never met a private investigator before. How do you do? I am Tomas Varnas, and I'm very pleased to meet you.'

He holds out his hand, and we shake hands. Wrong name, I think. Not the name on the door. But this *is* the Lithuanian boyfriend.

'Shirley Homes. Pleased to meet you too,' I say. 'I'm sorry about this. But I need to talk to you. Carrie's mother—'

'Of course,' says Tomas. 'I understand. Please – sit down. Can I get you some coffee?'

He and Carrie make coffee, and we all sit down round a table. Tomas looks at me, smiling.

'So,' he says. 'You want to ask me questions, so you can tell Carrie's mother all about me. I am very happy about that. What do you want to know? Shall I begin?'

So I listen to the story of Tomas Varnas's life. He is nineteen years old, and comes from Vilnius in Lithuania. He came to London six months ago because he wants to start a business. His family make linen cloth in Vilnius, and Tomas wants to sell it in England. At the moment he's working Monday to Friday in a hospital because he needs the money. But he's selling linen in the street market on Saturdays. Business is good, and is getting better every week.

Carrie wants to tell me more about it. 'It's beautiful linen, you know. The best in the world. I'm learning all about it.' She's excited, I can see it in her green eyes.

Tomas is smiling. 'Carrie is very good with the colours of the linen,' he says. 'She wants to work with me. And she's good at business too – very good. Better than me.'

He puts the back of his hand against Carrie's face, just a touch, a very gentle touch, and smiles into her eyes. She looks up at him, and the love in her eyes is clear. For a second or two the world stops for them. These two young people are very much in love.

Carrie looks at me again. 'Everybody wants to wear clothes made of linen now, you see. So our business is going to get bigger.'

'Lots of hard work,' says Tomas. 'But we're young, we can work hard, no problem about that. But we do have one problem.' He looks at Carrie. 'Your family.'

'Oh, that!' Carrie says. 'Not important. I don't need them. We're fine without them.'

'Not so,' Tomas says gently. 'Your mother is unhappy, your little brother is unhappy, and your father too.'

'No, he isn't! My father is a horrible man! We have arguments all the time. Every day he tells me, "do this,

Tomas is selling linen in the street market on Saturdays.

don't do that, do this." *He's* always right, and *I'm* always wrong! Always! He *never* listens to me. He doesn't understand me, he doesn't *want* to understand me. He's just *horrible* . . .'

'Shhh, shhh,' Tomas says. 'When people are angry, sometimes they say bad things. Maybe they don't really think that. You and your father have a lot of arguments, and you both get angry and say things.'

'Yes, but . . .' Carrie says.

I sit and listen. This is not their first argument, and it's not going to be their last one. It's interesting to listen to them. Tomas is very gentle with Carrie, but he's strong too. He's in love, but he still thinks clearly.

'Er, excuse me,' I say. 'I'm still here, you know.'

They look at me. Tomas laughs. 'Sorry!' he says. 'We talk about this often. In the end, Carrie must go back home. She knows that.'

'No, I don't!' says Carrie. 'I'm not going back home. No way!'

'But Carrie – you can't cut your family out of your life. Family is important. *My* family is important to me. And I want you to have your family too . . . to be friends with your mother, and your father. And your little brother!'

They're off again. I'm trying not to smile. This argument is going to run and run. I think Tomas is good for Carrie.

'Well, I'm done here,' I say. 'It was good to meet you, Tomas. I can tell Mrs Williams about you now. And, well . . . good luck to both of you.'

Carrie smiles. 'Thanks, Shirley. Can I call you Shirley? Ant and Janice said you were all right. I sent mum a text last night, you know.'

Tomas stands up too. 'I must get home now,' he says.

I stare at him, surprised. 'Home? You live here, in this apartment. Don't you?'

'No, no, no,' Tomas says. 'Of course not! Carrie is fifteen. We cannot marry before she is sixteen years old. It is against the law. So of course I don't live here. It is not correct.'

'But this is your apartment—?'

'No, no,' Tomas says again. 'It's my sister's apartment. Carrie lives here with my sister, Ruta Varnaite. She's

They're off again. I'm trying not to smile.

working late tonight. I have a room with a friend near Putney Bridge.'

I'm very surprised. I sit down again and look at Carrie. 'Why didn't you tell me? Everybody thinks you're living with Tomas.'

Carrie doesn't look pleased. 'Well, I didn't tell them that. But my dad always thinks the worst. And sometimes my mum too. But we can get married next year, when I'm sixteen.'

Tomas laughs. He pulls her hair, gently. 'Sixteen is still very young to get married. We can wait. I want to know your family first, and you want to know my family.'

'Yes, I really want to meet your family,' Carrie says. 'But you don't want to meet mine, you really don't.'

Tomas pulls her hair again, not so gently this time. 'Of course I do. I want to talk to your father, I want him to like me. We have all the time in the world, Carrie. Let's just take our time, eh?'

Carrie tries to look angry, then she laughs, and puts her arms around him.

Tomas and I leave the house together. He walks with me to my car.

'I'm sorry about Mr Williams,' he says. 'I think he loves Carrie a lot. Maybe I can meet him and talk to him one day. But Mrs Williams doesn't need to be afraid for Carrie. Please tell her that.'

'Of course,' I say. I've got a lot to say to Mrs Williams. Tomas and I shake hands again, and say goodbye.

I drive back to my office, and check my messages. There's a message from Saheed. *Call me about the Lithuanian boyfriend.*

I send him a text.

> Found the boyfriend, thanks.
> And the girl. All well, no problems.
> Easy case, nothing horrible.
> But thanks for the help!
> SH

A text comes back from Saheed at once.

> Oh, thanks a lot! I made 12 phone calls
> for you, all for nothing! Next time, YOU
> can help ME!
> SP

Oh dear! Saheed is not pleased. I often need his help so I must be nice to him. I send him another text.

> Sorry! Really really sorry!
> Can I buy you a beer tonight?
> SH

A text comes back from him.

> OK. The King's Arms, by the river.
> 9 o'clock this evening. See you.
> SP

CHAPTER 5

A foot in the door

Saheed and I have a beer together, and I tell him all about the Lithuanian case.

'A father–daughter problem, eh?' says Saheed. 'Well, I know all about difficult fathers.'

Saheed is from an Indian family. He and his sister Leila have their problems with a difficult father too. But Saheed never talks about his problems. He just does his job. He's a good detective.

'So. You did a good job there. A happy ending,' says Saheed.

'Yes, and no,' I say. 'One more thing to do.'

We finish our beer and leave.

'Say hi to Leila for me,' I say. Leila is my best friend. She's a lawyer. Leila, Saheed, and I have a lot of arguments about the law, and the police, and private investigators. We have a good time. I'm always right, of course.

∎

The next day is Saturday. I do some work on my laptop in the office, and think about the Lithuanian case. How many young men are there like Tomas Varnas?

I think about it some more, then I leave, and walk to the Williams' house. It's not far from my office.

Mrs Williams opens the door, sees me, and tries to shut the door again. But my foot is in the door . . .

'Can I come in, Mrs Williams?' I say. 'Just for a minute.'

'It's Saturday. My husband's at home,' Edith Williams says. 'Please speak quietly! Look, I've got your money ready – here it is. And thank you, thank you. Carrie is

My foot is in the door . . .

texting me every day now, so I know she's all right. Please go now, please don't—'

'Who's that at the door, Edith?' It's a man's voice, a big strong voice.

'Oh, nobody,' Mrs Williams says quickly, but I'm inside the door now, and looking at Mr Williams.

'Oh, hello,' he says. 'Who are you?'

'Shirley Homes, private investigator. How do you do? Your wife wanted me to find Carrie. And to talk to her boyfriend.'

'What!' Mr Williams turns to his wife. 'What did I say to you, Edith?' he shouts. 'We're finished with that girl! We don't speak to her, we don't talk about her, we—'

'And it's good news, Mr Williams!' I use my head teacher voice again. He's still shouting at his wife, so I shout too. And smile and smile.

'Yes, it's very good news, Mr Williams. Your daughter Carrie is alive and well and living in London. And she has a wonderful boyfriend!'

Mr Williams stops shouting and stares at me. Behind him I can just see Darren's head. He's looking round a door, with big eyes.

'Carrie's boyfriend is a very nice young man. His name is Tomas Varnas, he's nineteen years old, he's a hard worker, he's kind . . .'

'He's a foreigner,' Mr Williams says angrily.

'You have a problem with foreigners?' I say.

Mr Williams is staring at me angrily.

Mrs Williams closes her eyes. She's waiting for something . . . What? A lot of bad language about foreigners from her husband?

I look at Mr Williams again, but he isn't saying anything. He's just staring at me angrily. And suddenly, I understand. His problem isn't with foreigners, it's with his daughter. He *wants* to know that Carrie is all right, he *wants* to hear about her boyfriend, he *wants* to see her, to have her back home. But he can't find the words. He just can't say it.

I speak quickly. 'Tomas is a very nice young man.' I say it again, it's an important message. 'He works hard, he's doing two jobs, and he's going to make a good life for him and Carrie. He speaks very good English, and he's kind, and he's funny, but he's strong too. He thinks family is important, and he wants Carrie to come back home, to be friends with her mother, her father, her brother . . .'

All three of them are listening to me now. Darren has a big smile on his face.

'Oh, and Carrie is living with Tomas's sister, not with Tomas, you know. Carrie wants to get married when she's sixteen next year, but Tomas wants to wait. He wants to meet the family, and he wants Carrie to meet his family. So you see – Tomas Varnas is a good man, a really good man. He's a boyfriend to please any father in Britain, Mr Williams.'

Carrie's father opens his mouth, and closes it again. He still can't find the words.

'So now you know all about him, Mr Williams. Meet him. Talk to him. Ask him to Sunday lunch.'

I turn to Mrs Williams. 'Do you usually have Sunday lunch, you know, that wonderful British meal? All foreigners love it.'

'Er, yes,' she says. 'I . . . er . . . yes, I always do a nice Sunday lunch.'

'Well, there you are then,' I say. I smile around at everybody. 'Sunday lunch. That's a good way to meet your daughter's boyfriend.'

I take my money from Mrs Williams, give Darren a big smile and a wave, and walk to the front door. Nobody's shouting, nobody's crying. So far, so good.

'Have a nice day, everyone!' I say, and close the door behind me.

CHAPTER 6

A surprise visitor

The next three weeks are busy. I have a new case to work on, and I'm out of the office nearly every day. I don't like the client very much, but the case is an interesting one.

On Saturday morning I'm in the office again. I have a lot of emails to write, so I'm not pleased when my doorbell rings.

The computer screen shows me a man at the door. Well, well, well, what a surprise! I hit the 'open door' button, and the man comes in.

The door opens and the man comes in.

'Mr Williams, good morning. How are you?' I say. What does he want?

'Morning, Ms Homes.' He's not friendly, he's not unfriendly. He looks around my little room.

'Nice office,' he says. 'Can you see the river from your window?' He walks to the window, looks out. *What does he want?* Does he just want to talk about my office? Maybe the weather's next . . .

'It's colder today,' he says. 'Autumn's coming.'

I wait.

He comes away from the window. 'Can I sit down? Just for a minute.'

'Of course. Please,' I say.

Now he looks at me. 'I just wanted to say . . . Well, you were right about Tomas Varnas. He's a fine young man. I like him a lot.'

'Well, that's great, Mr Williams. I'm very pleased. So, tell me. What happened?'

He smiles, and gets comfortable in my best chair. He wants to tell me all about it.

'We asked him to Sunday lunch. Like you said. And he and Carrie came to lunch, and stayed all day. Lots to talk about.' He laughs. 'Me and Carrie have an argument, of course, but we always do. Tom – I call him Tom now, you see – is very good for Carrie. He doesn't get excited, and angry, like Carrie does. And Carrie listens to him.' He laughs again. 'She never listens to me!'

'*We asked Tomas to Sunday lunch.*'

I smile, and say something about the father–daughter thing.

'So Carrie's back home with us now. Tom comes round every evening, of course. And weekends. He's out with Darren now, playing football. Darren thinks he's wonderful!'

'Tomas is a big brother for Darren,' I say.

'That's right,' says Mr Williams. 'Oh, and Carrie's back at school too. She wants to do business studies, then she can help Tom with his linen business. She's got a good head for business, you know.' He laughs. 'My little Carrie – a businesswoman!'

He stands up. 'Well, you're busy, I can see that. I just wanted to tell you about Tom.'

'I like good news, Mr Williams,' I say. 'And it was good of you to come.' I walk with him to the door.

At the door, he says, 'You helped my family a lot. Maybe one day you need help. Just call me.' He gives me his business card. 'Anything. Who knows?'

Who knows? I'm going to remember those words . . .

GLOSSARY

age the number of years somebody has lived

apartment a group of rooms for living in, on one floor of a house or building

argument talking angrily with someone because you do not agree

awesome *(informal)* very good, great, enjoyable

backpack a bag that you carry on your back

blond (of hair colour) a light gold colour

business your work, your job; also making and selling things

card (business card) a small piece of card with your name, address, phone number, etc. on it

case a problem or a question that needs an answer

check to find out what is there (e.g. check your email)

client a person who pays another person for help

correct behaving in a way that follows accepted rules

crazy very angry

dangerous something dangerous can hurt you

detective a person whose job is to find out who did a crime

doorbell a bell on a house door which you push to tell the people inside you are there

drug an illegal chemical substance that people take because it makes them happy or excited

follow to go after somebody or something

foreigner a person from another country

funny making you laugh or smile

gentle quiet and kind

glasses you wear glasses to help your eyes to see better

great very good; very large

guys *(plural, informal)* used when speaking to a group of people

horrible very bad, unpleasant; **horribly** *(adv)* very

idiot a stupid person

kind friendly and good to other people

laptop a small computer that you can carry

law (the law) all the rules of a country

lawyer a person who knows the law and helps people in trouble

linen a kind of strong cloth made from flax

missing lost, or not in the usual place

private investigator a detective who is not in the police, and who has private clients

problem something that is difficult, or that worries you

really in fact, actually; very or very much

report information (written or spoken) about something that has happened

shout to speak very loudly

stare to look at somebody or something for a long time

strong not easily frightened or influenced; powerful

surprise how you feel when something unexpected happens

surprised *(adj)* feeling or showing surprise

text *(v & n)* a message in writing you send on a mobile phone

touch to put your hand or finger on something or somebody

trouble difficulty, problems, or worry; **be in trouble** to have problems because you have done something wrong or silly

unfriendly not friendly

unhappy not happy

wig wearing a 'hat' of hair which is not your own hair

ACTIVITIES

Before Reading

1 **Read the back cover of the book, and the introduction on the first page. How much do you know now about the story? Tick one box for each sentence.**

	YES	NO
1 Shirley Homes is a detective.	☐	☐
2 Shirley Homes works for the police.	☐	☐
3 She has a university degree from Harvard, USA.	☐	☐
4 She is working on a missing persons case.	☐	☐
5 The missing person is a fifteen-year-old girl.	☐	☐
6 Shirley has a Lithuanian boyfriend.	☐	☐
7 Carrie Williams left home fifteen weeks ago.	☐	☐

2 **What is going to happen in this story? Can you guess? Choose words to complete these sentences.**

1 Shirley Homes *finds / does not find* Carrie Williams.

2 Carrie Williams is *dead / alive*.

3 Shirley looks for Carrie in *Lithuania / London*.

4 Carrie is living in *Lithuania / London*.

5 Carrie's boyfriend is a *good / bad* man.

6 Carrie *is / is not* living with her boyfriend.

7 At the end of the story, Carrie *goes home to her family / marries her boyfriend*.

8 By the end of story, the boyfriend *is in prison / is a friend of Carrie's family*.

ACTIVITIES

While Reading

Read chapters 1 and 2. Who is who? Complete the sentences with people from this list. One word is needed twice.

boyfriend / brother / detective / father / friends / mother

1 Carrie left home after an argument with her _____.
2 The argument was about Carrie's _____.
3 Carrie's _____ wants Shirley to find Carrie.
4 Carrie's _____ doesn't want to see Carrie again.
5 Carrie's little _____ is very unhappy about all this.
6 Shirley talks to some of Carrie's _____ from school.
7 Shirley asks her friend Saheed, a police _____, for help.

Before you read chapter 3, try to guess what happens. Choose one answer to this question.

1 Who comes to meet Shirley in the café?
   a) Carrie and Ant   c) Carrie
   b) Carrie and her boyfriend   d) Nobody

Read chapters 3 and 4. Who says or texts this? Who are they texting or speaking to?

1 'I don't need my family. I have a new life now.'
2 'Always change your mobile when you don't want people to find you.'

3 'Saw C today. She's fine.'
4 'When people are angry, sometimes they say bad things.'
5 'I sent mum a text last night, you know.'
6 'Of course I don't live here. It is not correct.'
7 'We have all the time in the world.'
8 'Easy case, nothing horrible. But thanks for the help!'
9 'I made 12 phone calls for you, all for nothing!'

Before you read chapter 5, *A foot in the door*, try to guess what happens. Choose one answer to the question.

1 How does Shirley tell Mrs Williams about Carrie's boyfriend?
   a) She sends her a text message.
   b) She phones her.
   c) She goes to her house.
   d) She writes her a letter.
   e) She sends her an email.

Before you read chapter 6, *A surprise visitor*, can you guess what happens? Choose answers to the questions.

1 Do the Williams family invite Tomas Varnas to Sunday lunch? YES / NO
2 Does Carrie go back to live at home? YES / NO
3 Who comes to Shirley's office to tell her all about it?
   Carrie / Mrs Williams / Mr Williams / Tomas / Darren / Ant / Janice / Kim

ACTIVITIES

After Reading

1 **Match these parts of sentences together, and choose the best linking word to join them.**

1 Mrs Williams wants Shirley to look for Carrie, . . .

2 Shirley takes Darren for a pizza . . .

3 Shirley doesn't want Carrie to see her on the bus, . . .

4 Carrie wants to get married . . .

5 Tomas wants to meet Carrie's family . . .

6 Shirley goes to the Williams' house . . .

7 Mr Williams really cares about his daughter, . . .

8 *after / before* he and Carrie get married.

9 *because / so* she changes her clothes, and puts on a wig.

10 *and / but* he can't find the words to say it.

11 *but / because* she doesn't want her husband to know.

12 *before / when* she is sixteen.

13 *so / because* she wants Mr Williams to hear about Tomas.

14 *because / so* he helped her with Carrie's school friends.

2 **After meeting Shirley, Ant sends Carrie a text. Complete her text with these words (one word for each gap).**

alive, cries, investigator, meet, mum, name, OK, school, tell

Hey! We met this private _____ today in the street outside _____. Her _____ is Shirley Homes. She's _____, we liked her. She wants to _____ you tomorrow or the day after. Café Nero, 18.30. She says your _____ can't sleep and _____ all the time. Shirley just wants to know you're _____ and well. Then she can _____ your mum.

3 Use the clues to complete this crossword with words from the story. Then find the hidden eight-letter word in the crossword.

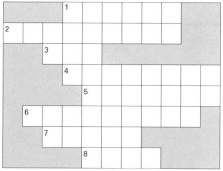

1 Tomas wants to meet Carrie's _____.

2 Tomas is Carrie's _____.

3 When Shirley follows Carrie, she wears a blond _____.

4 Carrie is going to do _____ studies at school.

5 There are about 1,000 _____ persons reports every day.

6 Tomas is from Lithuania, so in London he's a _____.

7 Tomas's family make _____ cloth.

8 After Shirley talks to Carrie, Carrie sends her mother a _____.

What is the hidden word? _____ Does every family have these? What do *you* think?

4 Here is a new illustration for the story. Find the best place in the story to put the picture, and answer these questions.

The picture goes on page _____.

1 Who is this?
2 What is she doing?
3 Why is she doing this?

Now write a caption for the illustration.

Caption: _____

5 **Shirley talked to her friend Saheed a few weeks later. Put their conversation in the right order, and write in the speakers' names. Shirley speaks first (number 3).**

1 _____ 'That's right, but that wasn't the end of the story.'

2 _____ *[laughs]* 'That great British meal! And did he?'

3 _____ 'You remember my Lithuanian case, Saheed?'

4 _____ 'And how *did* you hear about all this, Shirley?'

5 _____ 'Yes. Tomas went to lunch, and now everybody in the Williams family loves him! He plays football with the little brother, and the girl is back at school, studying hard. It's all wonderful, I hear!'

6 _____ 'Yes, I do. Last month, wasn't it? You found the missing girl, and the boyfriend was a nice guy.'

7 _____ 'The girl's father didn't like foreigners, but I told him to meet the boy, and ask him to Sunday lunch.'

8 _____ 'A happy dad, eh? That's nice. We don't get many happy endings like that in the police, I can tell you.'

9 _____ 'Mr Williams came to my office. He thinks Tomas is a fine young man, and he wanted to tell me that.'

10 _____ 'Oh? What happened after that, then?'

6 **How did you feel about the people in this story? Put a name in the first gap, then finish the sentences in your own words.**

1 I felt sorry for _____ *because* / *when* _____.

2 I did not feel sorry for _____ *because* / *when* _____.

3 I liked _____ *because* / *when* _____.

4 I did not like _____ *because* / *when* _____.

ABOUT THE AUTHOR

Jennifer Bassett has worked in English Language Teaching since 1972. She has been a teacher, teacher trainer, editor, and materials writer, and has taught in England, Greece, Spain, and Portugal. She is the Series Editor of the *Oxford Bookworms Library* of graded readers, and has written more than twenty original and retold stories for the series, including *The Phantom of the Opera*, *One-Way Ticket*, *The President's Murderer*, *The Omega Files*, all at Stage 1, and *William Shakespeare* at Stage 2.

Two of her adaptations, *Rabbit-Proof Fence* (Stage 3) and *Love Among the Haystacks* (Stage 2), have won Language Learner Literature Awards from the Extensive Reading Foundation <www.erfoundation.com>, and five of her other titles have been finalists for the Awards. She has also created a new sub-series called *Bookworms World Stories*, which are collections of short stories written in English from around the world. With H.G. Widdowson, she is series co-adviser of the *Oxford Bookworms Collection*, volumes of unadapted short stories for advanced learners.

Jennifer lives and works in Devonshire, in south-west England, and loves walking on Dartmoor, which is the setting for the famous Sherlock Holmes story, *The Hound of the Baskervilles*. She enjoys reading all kinds of detective stories, including the Conan Doyle stories. Sherlock Holmes is probably the most famous private detective in the world, although he is not, of course, the great-great-grandfather of Shirley Homes!

OXFORD BOOKWORMS LIBRARY

Classics • Crime & Mystery • Factfiles • Fantasy & Horror
Human Interest • Playscripts • Thriller & Adventure
True Stories • World Stories

The OXFORD BOOKWORMS LIBRARY provides enjoyable reading in English, with a wide range of classic and modern fiction, non-fiction, and plays. It includes original and adapted texts in seven carefully graded language stages, which take learners from beginner to advanced level. An overview is given on the next pages.

All Stage 1 titles are available as audio recordings, as well as over eighty other titles from Starter to Stage 6. All Starters and many titles at Stages 1 to 4 are specially recommended for younger learners. Every Bookworm is illustrated, and Starters and Factfiles have full-colour illustrations.

The OXFORD BOOKWORMS LIBRARY also offers extensive support. Each book contains an introduction to the story, notes about the author, a glossary, and activities. Additional resources include tests and worksheets, and answers for these and for the activities in the books. There is advice on running a class library, using audio recordings, and the many ways of using Oxford Bookworms in reading programmes. Resource materials are available on the website <www.oup.com/bookworms>.

The *Oxford Bookworms Collection* is a series for advanced learners. It consists of volumes of short stories by well-known authors, both classic and modern. Texts are not abridged or adapted in any way, but carefully selected to be accessible to the advanced student.

You can find details and a full list of titles in the *Oxford Bookworms Library Catalogue* and *Oxford English Language Teaching Catalogues*, and on the website <www.oup.com/bookworms>.

THE OXFORD BOOKWORMS LIBRARY GRADING AND SAMPLE EXTRACTS

STARTER • 250 HEADWORDS

present simple – present continuous – imperative –
can/cannot, must – going to (future) – simple gerunds …

Her phone is ringing – but where is it?

Sally gets out of bed and looks in her bag. No phone. She looks under the bed. No phone. Then she looks behind the door. There is her phone. Sally picks up her phone and answers it. *Sally's Phone*

STAGE 1 • 400 HEADWORDS

… past simple – coordination with *and, but, or* –
subordination with *before, after, when, because, so* …

I knew him in Persia. He was a famous builder and I worked with him there. For a time I was his friend, but not for long. When he came to Paris, I came after him – I wanted to watch him. He was a very clever, very dangerous man. *The Phantom of the Opera*

STAGE 2 • 700 HEADWORDS

… present perfect – *will* (future) – (*don't*) *have to, must not, could* –
comparison of adjectives – simple *if* clauses – past continuous –
tag questions – *ask/tell* + infinitive …

While I was writing these words in my diary, I decided what to do. I must try to escape. I shall try to get down the wall outside. The window is high above the ground, but I have to try. I shall take some of the gold with me – if I escape, perhaps it will be helpful later. *Dracula*

STAGE 3 • 1000 HEADWORDS

… should, may – present perfect continuous – *used to* – past perfect –
causative – relative clauses – indirect statements …

Of course, it was most important that no one should see
Colin, Mary, or Dickon entering the secret garden. So Colin
gave orders to the gardeners that they must all keep away
from that part of the garden in future. *The Secret Garden*

STAGE 4 • 1400 HEADWORDS

… past perfect continuous – passive (simple forms) –
would conditional clauses – indirect questions –
relatives with *where/when* – gerunds after prepositions/phrases …

I was glad. Now Hyde could not show his face to the world
again. If he did, every honest man in London would be proud
to report him to the police. *Dr Jekyll and Mr Hyde*

STAGE 5 • 1800 HEADWORDS

… future continuous – future perfect –
passive (modals, continuous forms) –
would have conditional clauses – modals + perfect infinitive …

If he had spoken Estella's name, I would have hit him. I was so
angry with him, and so depressed about my future, that I could
not eat the breakfast. Instead I went straight to the old house.
Great Expectations

STAGE 6 • 2500 HEADWORDS

… passive (infinitives, gerunds) – advanced modal meanings –
clauses of concession, condition

When I stepped up to the piano, I was confident. It was as if I
knew that the prodigy side of me really did exist. And when I
started to play, I was so caught up in how lovely I looked that
I didn't worry how I would sound. *The Joy Luck Club*

BOOKWORMS • CRIME & MYSTERY • STAGE 1
Sherlock Holmes and the Duke's Son

SIR ARTHUR CONAN DOYLE

Retold by Jennifer Bassett

Dr Huxtable has a school for boys in the north of England. When the Duke of Holdernesse decides to send his young son there, that is good news for the school. The Duke is a very important person, and Dr Huxtable is happy to have his son in the school.

But two weeks later Dr Huxtable is the unhappiest man in England. Why? And why does he take the train down to London and go to Baker Street? Why does he need the help of the famous detective Sherlock Holmes?

Because someone has kidnapped the Duke's son . . .

BOOKWORMS • THRILLER & ADVENTURE • STAGE 1
Goodbye, Mr Hollywood

JOHN ESCOTT

Nick Lortz is sitting outside a café in Whistler, a village in the Canadian mountains, when a stranger comes and sits next to him. She's young, pretty, and has a beautiful smile. Nick is happy to sit and talk with her.

But why does she call Nick 'Mr Hollywood'? Why does she give him a big kiss when she leaves? And who is the man at the next table – the man with short white hair?

Nick learns the answers to these questions three long days later – in a police station on Vancouver Island.